Kate Liberty

Homemade Dog Treats Recipes

A Complete Cookbook with over 30 Easy & Delicious Homemade Dog Treats Recipes

Copyright © 2020 publishing.

All rights reserved.

Author: Kate Liberty

No part of this publication may be reproduced, distributed or transmitted in any form or by any means, including photocopying recording or other electronic or mechanical methods or by any information storage and retrieval system without the prior written permission of the publisher, except in the case of brief quotation embodies in critical reviews and certain other non-commercial uses permitted by copyright law.

Table of Contents

About Homemade Dog Treats 5

Homemade Dog Treat Recipes Why Use Them 12

Discover the Money Saving Reasons Behind Homemade Dog Treats Recipes 23

Easy Homemade Dog Treats... 27

Healthy Herbal Homemade Dog Treats 38

Tips in Making Homemade Dog Food Treats 41

33 Delicious Homemade Dog Treats Recipes 47

Homemade Dog Treats Vs Store Bought 107

About Homemade Dog Treats

Homemade dog treats may seem like a lot of work for some people.

Others like the idea of making their own dog food or treats but are not sure of the recipes and ingredients. But dogs from both families would love homemade treats!

Why you should make your own dog treats

So why do you want to take the time to make your own dog treats and snacks? You will have much more flexibility in that you feed your dog if you have more control.

You can avoid allergies or other food concerns.

You will have unlimited flavor combinations instead of limiting yourself to what producers choose. You can modify recipes to meet your dog's nutritional needs, such as replacing low-fat peanut butter.

How to save time by making treats for dogs

When you make large batches or different types of homemade dog treats, you won't need to play Doggie Chef as often. Freeze individual treats or single-dose meals on a cookie tray.

Then, once completely frozen, you can transfer them to a plastic bag for storage. Since they are frozen individually, they will not stick together, and you can simply move some of them to the refrigerator if necessary and let them thaw overnight.

What to look for in recipes for dogs

There are several key things to consider when choosing a dog treat or dog food recipe. Depending on your culinary skills, just choose or skip the recipes according to the following tips. Of course, if you feel comfortable making replacements, then you have even more options.

Choose recipes that -

Focus on the ingredients your dog likes

Sounds appealing to you (it's not that you're going to eat!)

Among the plots that your dog prefers: soft, crispy, large, small, cold, room temperature, etc.

Avoid recipes that contain ingredients that your dog doesn't like and are allergic to.

When choosing a cookbook or compiling home treatment recipes for dogs, you want enough options without feeling overwhelmed. Fifty recipes would be the minimum, while three hundred or more is really too much.

Between one hundred and two hundred is a good number, because then you have options and many varieties, but not so much that you cannot decide which ones to try.

Your dog needs to eat, and you are responsible for his health and have to pay for both. Why not do everything possible to give your dog healthy food and treats that will help maintain its health and reduce possible veterinary expenses? This is really a win-win situation for you and your dog!

Homemade Recipes for Dogs Give You Flexibility

Using homemade dog recipes gives you unlimited flexibility in the quality and variety of dog treats you provide to your dogs. Chicken, beef, lamb, and rice are some of the most popular flavors of commercially prepared dog treats and food, but your flavor combinations are unlimited when you use your homemade dog recipes. You can use peanut butter and honey to create desserts that do not include meat, or that can replace the meat you choose in your home dog treatment recipes.

Many traditional homemade dog treats recipes include meats such as chicken, veal and lamb, but when you create your own homemade dog treats, you have the option to replace other meats in the recipe, as long as the meats are safe for your dog. Homemade dog treats are usually cheaper than commercially prepared dog treats, but the flexibility of these recipes saves you additional costs. You have the option to buy meats that are on sale or have discounted prices when you follow a dog house treat recipe. You also have the option to reduce or increase the meat content to meet the tastes and needs of your dog.

Another advantage of home treatment recipes for dogs is that they can be tailored to your dog's nutritional needs. Recipes that require peanut butter can use low-fat peanut butter if treats are prepared for an overweight dog. You can also remove any ingredient to which your dog has a known allergy. The flexibility available in home treatment recipes for dogs allows you to create a treatment suitable for all dogs.

Tips on Dog Treatment Recipes

Here is a very simple way to save money and your pet's health by cooking your own recipes of dog treats.

Dogs can eat a wide range of vegetables, including tomatoes, carrots and pumpkin. When you cook your delicacies, you can experiment with different ingredients. Remember, Fido is much less demanding than most people!

You can also add things like flaxseed to your pet's delights for a delicious hazelnut flavor and lots of healthy omega-3s.

It doesn't have to be complicated or time-consuming, but there are some things you need to know.

1) Dog treats can be made from meat or wheat. For example, you can cut liver and bake for a meat treat, or you can take flour and blender and mix cookies with pumpkin or grated chicken.

2) You can make decorative delights with fancy cookie cutters and carob, or iced yogurt sprinkled on top, or you can make them simple. A simple way is to make a dough, roll it into a trunk and freeze it. When it is frozen, you can cut the dog's processing in turns and bake in the oven!

3) There are some ingredients that can make a dog really sick if they eat them. Raisins and grapes should be left out of the treatment recipes for dogs. A little onion or garlic is fine, but going easy as much can close the kidneys. Chocolate is certainly a step because it can do the same.

Cooking Dog treats recipes is a great way to ensure that your pet is always treated healthy without toxic chemicals and animal by-products.

In addition, you get the look of pure joy on your puppy's face when he realizes that you have cooked something for him. You think I'm joking, try it and look.

So, you have it, three tips on how to create your own dog treatment recipes. What are you waiting for? Your dog is waiting!

Raw Homemade Dog Treats

Homemade dog treats should not involve baking. There is a growing trend in the diet of dogs —a raw diet consisting of raw meat and vegetables. A popular version of this diet is known as the bones and raw food diet (BARF). This diet emphasizes your dog's feeding, only natural foods that have not been cooked or otherwise processed. You can follow this diet's principles to provide your dog with homemade delicacies that do not involve much work.

The barf diet includes the use of raw and fleshy bones and contains elements such as chicken wings, neck and back. It is important to note that while it is safe to give your dog raw chicken that includes bones, it is not safe to give them chicken that has been cooked that includes bones. The bones are softened during the cooking process, making them brittle and a choking risk for dogs. However, raw chicken bones are not likely to crumble and create this danger and are therefore safe to give to dogs.

Buying a bag of frozen chicken wings is a way to provide your dog with incredibly simple homemade delicacies. These delicacies can be as simple as removing a chicken wing or two from the freezer and distributing them to your dog.

Homemade Dog Treat Recipes Why Use Them

Homemade dog treat recipes can be elusive; however, they convey numerous advantages once they are discovered. For some individuals, they may not understand that they have to utilize these when they are making some homemade dog treats. When an individual acknowledges why they have to utilize these, however, they can see exactly how significant these things can be.

One motivation to utilize this is on the grounds that they can enable an individual to recognize what sort of food they can place into the treat. Presently on the off chance that you resemble a great many people, you appreciate eating chocolate. Nonetheless, regardless of whether your dog is asking all that he needs, he can't have this decent delicious treat. Giving them this kind of pleasant scrumptious tidbit could end up being hurtful to the dog even to the point of murdering them. In this way, utilizing these books can permit an individual to recognize what they can place into the treat.

Another motivation to utilize the book is because it can give thoughts that somebody may have never pondered. So rather than agonizing over what an individual will make for a treat every night, they can discover the books that will furnish them with all the thoughts they need to have.

Something different that an individual can understand by utilizing these are that they often incorporate various recipes that they can utilize. While a few people may not understand that they can run out of thoughts without a book, the book can, for the most part, help work the memory of various ones. Then on the off chance that you resemble many great people, it is conceivable to bookmark the ones that the dog adored the most and maintain a strategic distance from the ones that they didn't care about that well in the wake of attempting them.

An individual may find that these can help shield them from giving the dog food that they love that could hurt them. When purchasing the things at the store, an individual may think they are giving the dog something great, yet they have to understand that the things made there are often made in business mass bundles, which could prompt a slip in quality.

The reviews won't influence these things since they are made in the home. A couple of years back, numerous individuals may review the monster dog food reviews. Well, those are still happening even today. Nonetheless, by making these things at home, an individual won't need to stress over any influenced the treats that they are providing for the dog.

Having the option to locate the ideal homemade dog treat recipes can be a hard activity. In any case, it is a thing that holds numerous advantages for the dog and the proprietor themselves. A few people don't have a clue about the motivations to utilize these things and have to think about those reasons before they will at long last conclude that it was worthwhile to buy any books covering this point.

Incorporate Vitamin Supplements in Your Homemade Dog Treats Recipes

Homemade dog treats recipes enable you to incorporate nutrient supplements in your dog's eating routine. Like individuals, dogs often need supplements in their eating regimen, yet getting them to take pills can be a problem. Many dog proprietors resort to enclosing the supplement with a more attractive treat, yet a few dogs are basically too brilliant to even think about being tricked by this stunt.

There are additionally pill pockets accessible to shroud the treat, and even though they are successful, they can likewise be costly. One answer to the issue of taking care of your dog supplements is to remember them for your homemade dog treat recipes.

Glucosamine is a well-known supplement that advances joint health in dogs. Although this supplement is promptly accessible in business arranged dog foods and treats, fusing the supplement in your own homemade dog treat recipes can be a more conservative approach to remember these supplements for your dog's eating routine. You can utilize glucosamine tablets accessible for human utilization. However, numerous dogs will be hesitant to expend this massive pill. Notwithstanding, you could crush one suitable measure of glucosamine for each serving that your homemade dog treats recipes yields and consolidate the ground up supplement into the treats. This will make the supplement substantially more acceptable to your dog.

Healthy Home Dog Treat Recipes for Your Dog Companion

It is best to make your own dog treats so you know that the ingredients are safe and healthy for your dog companion. No need to be a great chef or even a good chef to make your own homemade dog treats. You can simply open your refrigerator and look for an aperitif that you would also like to eat.

An excellent quick and healthy treat for dogs would be turkey-based hot dogs or low-fat hot dogs. Just take a pack of hot dogs from the refrigerator, cut them into bite-sized pieces and lovingly feed your dog with this treat.

Vegetables can also be turned into delicacies for healthy dogs. Just cut green beans, carrots or potato cubes and give your dog a pleasure after playing "get the ball."

Chicken breasts cut into snacks —the size of a snack is excellent delicacies for dog food. Be sure not to give them chicken skin and especially chicken bones. Cooked chicken bones are not easy to digest; they will harm your dog.

On a hot spring or a summer day, ice cubes could be fun dog treats. Make ice cubes the day before by freezing meat or chicken broth in ice cubes.

There are also homemade recipes for dogs based on banana. Mix your favorite dough with chopped bananas and meat broth cubes for more flavors. Knead the dough and cut it into funny treats in the form of dog bones. Bake at 350 degrees for about 20 minutes, then cool before giving the treatment to your dog.

Another easy-to-do healthy treat is made from carrots. Boil and shred the carrots, mix with little oats for consistency, a few cubes of broth for more flavor, then make in a dough with a bit of flour, eggs and water. Do the same process, knead the dough, cut into bite-size shapes, bake and then serve!

An excellent refreshing gift for your dog is easy to make with activated charcoal and fresh mint. It is enough to mix brown rice flour with 1 tablespoon of activated charcoal, 3 tablespoons of canola oil, 1 egg, ½ cup of chopped fresh mint mixed with low-fat milk. Mix all the ingredients, knead and mold on a greased baking sheet. Cook for 30 minutes and cool before feeding the dog to your beloved dog.

The remaining turkey or chicken in the freezer could also be healthy delicacies for dog food. First, defrost the meat of turkey or chicken, cut the meat into cubes the size of a bite and serve your faithful dog.

It's so simple! No artificial ingredients, no harmful chemicals and no unknown ingredients that could have a negative effect on the overall health of your dogs. Timely treatment for dogs does not mean grabbing the most popular treatment on the shopping shelf. Homemade delicacies for dogs are made from natural ingredients that are very easy to prepare. These delicacies are not expensive at all. Another advantage is that you will not waste money by letting the leftovers go to a loss.

Homemade dog treatment recipes may seem like a great idea to create your own nutritious and affordable dog treats. Still, you also need to be extremely careful to make sure you do not give your dog everything that could be detrimental to his health. Ingredients such as cocoa, chocolate, grapes, raisins, onions and macadamia nuts are known to cause health problems when ingested by dogs. These ingredients cause problems ranging from kidney failure, anemia and irregular heartbeat, as well as neurological problems. To avoid these potentially deadly ingredients, you need to investigate each ingredient in the recipe.

It is imperative that you carefully search for ingredients in homemade dog treatment recipes to ensure that each ingredient is safe for dog consumption. It is recommended to use reliable sources for this important research. Published books, as well as websites run by highly regarded people, are excellent resources for finding ingredients in homemade recipes for dogs. If you do not find any specific information about the safety of a particular ingredient, it is advisable to show the list of ingredients to your veterinarian for advice. They may be able to tell you if the ingredients in your home dog treatment recipes are safe for your dog or not.

Making your own dog treats is getting famous among dog proprietors. For the individuals who don't have the foggiest idea how or don't have any desire to make their own, they can purchase homemade treats from individuals who maintain their own dog treat business. They make them and go to fairs, celebrations, and ranchers' business sectors to sell their items. It has become a blasting business for those ready to set aside the effort to make their own item.

What Are the Benefits of Homemade Dog Treats?

The most important advantage of dog proprietors is their pet's health. Since there are no additives or added substances, the supplement esteem is a lot higher. You also recognize what ingredients go into the homemade treats that help your pet if they have any health issues. If your dog is overweight, you can pick ingredients that are less stuffing. This additionally works with diabetes or delicate stomachs, or other food hypersensitivities.

Likewise, you can choose ingredients that will help your pet's prosperity, for example, a healthy coat and skin and to safeguard your dog's visual perception and hearing. You control your dog's food, which will give better sustenance to a more drawn out and healthier life.

Setting aside cash is another advantage of making your own dog treats. The American Kennel Club appraises that it costs around 25 hundred dollars to keep a pet each year. Search for approaches to decrease costs whenever you can. By picking food and treats that don't contain fillers and utilizing your own ingredients, you can set aside cash.

Tips for Making Homemade Dog Treats

Probably the best motivation to make your own dog treats is that you can utilize ingredients your dog likes. For example, pumpkin is a healthy, filling decision for treats, and it is low in calories. Dogs love pumpkin, which makes it gainful to use for overweight pets.

You can make homemade treats littler in size for pup preparation. You would prefer not to top them off; however, reward them when they follow your orders. Nutty spread is well known with all dogs and high in protein, building muscle and giving vitality to occupied little dogs.

On the off chance that you are new to heating homemade dog treats, pick a basic formula for your first experience. Gourmet treats are amusing to prepare after you've become acclimated to the thought; however, it can be hard for the tenderfoot. Pick a formula with ingredients that your dog prefers and isn't sensitive to and tail it as intently as could be expected under the circumstances.

Be mindful so as not to over-heat your treats. The preparing times may differ by the stove so check your treats infrequently. Recollect that homemade treats don't have additives, so they won't keep going insofar as locally acquired treats. On the off chance that the formula takes into consideration freezing, that will protect them longer.

Each pet proprietor needs to give the best consideration and food for their pet. They need to give them treats and prize them. By making homemade dog treats, you can give healthy decisions at a small amount of the expense for you. That will fulfill both you and your pet.

Avoid the Health Problems of Pets by Making Homemade Treats for Dogs

What is the difference between the dog treats you buy in the store, and the dog treats you make at home?

The biggest difference is that you know absolutely, 100% sure that the delicacies you make do not have harmful ingredients because you control what happens in them.

Even the best quality dog treats still suffer from quality control problems due to some food ingredients sewn with some preservatives or melamine. So why take unnecessary risks with your favorite pet? Take the time to learn how to create your own homemade delights.

Some people think it's too complicated to make dog treats. It is not more difficult, and in fact, many recipes are easier to prepare than a batch of simple old sugar cookies. In addition, your children will simply be happy to help you make homemade delights for the family pet. This is really an activity that the whole family can enjoy!

If your dog is a difficult eater or has allergies, you can adapt the ingredients and flavors to better meet your tastes and nutritional or health needs. No one knows better than you what your dog's preferences are: chicken flavor, liver flavor, or peanut butter flavor. You will definitely be a hero in your dog's eyes when you serve the best homemade specialties in the world!

Discover the Money Saving Reasons behind Homemade Dog Treats Recipes

A simple method to set aside cash is to make your own homemade dog scones for your dog with easy to make dog treats recipes. How does this set aside your cash?

We, as a whole, realize that by making anything ourselves, we can set aside cash. By doing a portion of the work, the expense is diminished, passing the investment funds legitimately to you!

That is a major advantage when you make dog treats homemade. As of now, you cook and eat for yourself, your loved ones; why not for your pet?

Ingredients - No More Specialty Formula Expense

Numerous individuals don't understand that homemade dog treats can be made with ingredients that you discover as of now on your kitchen rack. You can likewise control which ingredients go into the recipes. For instance, if your pup can't eat wheat, you can undoubtedly substitute an alternate fixing, for example, potato flour, in the formula. This sets aside your cash since you don't need to purchase any forte ingredients, which are consistently costly. It is that simple. By utilizing basic dog treats recipes, you set aside cash and no longer need to buy "unique equation" dog rolls. We, as a whole, realize these exceptional assortments are more costly.

No Need to Buy in Bulk to Save Money

Often stores tempt you to purchase food, treat or treat in mass sizes so as to spare a couple of pennies. Bid farewell to hauling gigantic boxes of dog items. At the point when stores offer limits for purchasing bigger amounts, we think we better snatch them quickly to set aside cash. Be that as it may, after you are home and the crate has been open for a couple of days, the dog treats can undoubtedly get stale. Discarding them resembles discarding cash! Where are the reserve funds in that? Purchasing bigger amounts likewise means dishing out more cash at once. Nobody ought to need to pay more cash in advance to spare a couple of pennies later on.

Invest Energy, Not Money on Your Pet

By utilizing straightforward dog treats recipes, you have the adaptability of making healthy food for your pet when you need it. No heading out to a claim to fame store or going around attempting to locate a unique brand. This gets a good deal on gas and spares time getting additional things done. Additional time implies you can be home playing with and making the most of your pet.

At the point when your canine needs more scones, you can rapidly prepare a new and scrumptious clump of yummy treats. Since the ingredients are new, the treats will taste better. Your dog will adore them, thus will you, when you understand how much cash you have spared.

Easy Homemade Dog Treats

Many dog proprietors make simple homemade dog treats as an approach to show their dog love or to use as motivation during preparing.

Dog treats made in your kitchen can go from easy to expand. Some require one moment or so utilizing crude, prepackaged or extra cooked foods and negligible ingredients, while others include getting ready and blending a few ingredients, then cooking or preparing them.

How about we start with the easiest treats initial, ones that comprise of just fixing.

Meat-Based Treats

Wieners or salami hotdogs that are cut into little pieces make extremely simple homemade dog treats. On the off chance that you are health cognizant, then search for the natural kind with low sodium. They are particularly useful for placing in a plastic baggie and giving out while preparing.

Solidified crude chicken wings can fill in as single treats for bigger dogs. They are additionally useful for helping keep a dog's teeth clean. (Crude chicken bones give off an impression of being alright for dogs to eat; it's the cooked kind that can fragment and cause issues).

Crude meat marrow or oxtail bones are likewise a decent treat that helps keep plaque off teeth. Bones territory in size from around two to four crawls in breadth so they can be taken care of to any measure dog.

Extra cooked meats can be cut up and taken care of too, and can likewise be useful for preparing purposes.

Our German Shepherd blend, Comet, often gets bits of jerky when we go climbing. It's extreme keeping his nose out of our rucksacks when we plunk down!

Organic Product or Vegetable Based

You can basically call these FREE homemade dog treats since your dog will probably just eat a little bit.

Cuts of leafy foods berries are things you may jump at the chance to attempt with your dog. Comet appreciates apple cuts on most days and will at times eat bits of banana, mango, melon, orange, peach or drink up strawberries, blackberries and blueberries. Be cautious with grapes and raisins as an excessive number of on the double can prompt kidney disappointment.

Spoonfuls of cooked sweet potato, green beans, peas, lentils, spinach, carrot, potato or squash are often valued. Consider sparing a portion of these vegetables after a supper with the goal that they can offer your dog a healthy treat the following day. Make certain to pound them up first.

Dairy or Egg Based

Touches of yogurt, curds, cream cheddar, or sharp cream often turn out well, as do cuts off every single, distinctive kind of cheeses.

Bits of cooked eggs or an extremely infrequent crude egg can likewise be utilized to let your dog think the individual in question is getting something unique. An or more is that eggs help a dog's skin and coat.

Straightforward Blends

A simple homemade dog treats formula to consolidate anything that shapes a spread with a portion of the above-mentioned.

For instance, you can put nutty spread or cream cheddar on any of the natural product things.

Likewise, consider including liverwurst or plate of mixed greens dressing (sufficiently only to give flavor) to an organic product, cut cheddar, hardboiled eggs, or bits of meat. I would recommend without sugar and sans sodium nutty spread if conceivable.

Despite the fact that you can take care of dog's things, for example, bread, saltines, entire bit corn, rice, and pasta, it is best to take care of these in exceptionally modest quantities since their stomach related framework isn't intended to deal with sugars. Additionally, if your dog eats a kibble-based eating routine, she/he will undoubtedly be accepting all that anyone could need from that food bunch as of now. Another issue with a portion of these foodstuffs is that they will stick to teeth in general and add to dental issues on the off chance that you don't brush your dog's teeth a while later.

All things considered; those are a portion of my thoughts for simple homemade dog treats. If your dog isn't accustomed to eating a specific kind of food, attempt him/her with a limited quantity first to ensure there are no hypersensitivities.

Reveal the Expert's secrets of the Best Dog Treats Recipes

A healthy, glad dog—isn't this your need as a pet proprietor? It isn't as troublesome as certain individuals will have you accept. It tends to be finished by drawing in the canine in standard exercise, setting up normal registration with an authorized vet, and keeping your dog in an eating regimen packed with fundamental nutrients and supplements.

So, what do you think about dog recipes? It is, all things considered, our duty to discover the things that enter our pet's frameworks. Keep in mind; homemade dog treats don't imply that you get whatever it is you find in your home. Not in the slightest degree. Did you realize that specific ingredients we people take are risky for dogs to ingest? This ought to stay away from no matter what.

Would you like to discover exceptional pastry treats you can give your dog? If you do, avoid macadamia nuts, chocolates, grapes, raisins, and caffeine since they have been demonstrated to be harmful to canines. An organic product is a vastly improved alternative (except for grapes). In any case, do eliminate the pits and seeds from organic products that you need to serve. These contain substances that trigger cyanide harming.

What about treats of the more flavorful kind? It will be gainful on the off chance that you keep handing the rundown of ingredients that have been tried to be dangerous to dogs. Anything liquor-based, onions and parts of the tomato plant are awful for dogs.

Liver—a magnificent wellspring of nutrient A, should just be given in littler sums. A lot of it will prompt bone issues.

Maybe your pet has a health confusion that warrants a particular change in accordance with his eating plan. Before taking care of your dog, any of the treats that appear to be acceptable, confirm with your vet.

Presently, there is no compelling reason to get scared by the rundown of dos and don'ts that appear to come up at you at each corner. As a matter of fact, as long as you most likely are aware of the food substances that you should avoid, arranging dog treats recipes are exceptionally basic. Actually, there is no compelling reason to restrict yourself. Be innovative in your menus! It should be an agreeable encounter that will harden your bond with your pet.

Since I am certain you have a charming pet, it may be troublesome not to indulge your dog with these luscious treats. However, it is significant that you don't go over the edge with treats of any sort. There are so numerous health inconveniences that accompany overweight dogs. Ask your vet the suggested weight for your specific dog and make it a highlighted screen of the calories he takes to keep up that weight.

Homemade dog treats are an incredible method to convey to your pet the amount they are adored and acknowledged. These great canine manifestations make certain to assemble your relationship with them your time and exertion will, without a doubt, be justified, despite all the trouble.

Easy Guide to Serving Natural Homemade Dog Treats

Despite the fact that business pet food is more helpful these days, an ever-increasing number of individuals, despite everything, discover time to get ready characteristic dog treats for their pets. Why would that be? Because it will be better for the health of the canines (even people besides) if there are fewer synthetic substances and additives in the food we take in.

Luckily regardless of what a few people say, homemade dog treats are not as trying as it might sound want to a few. In the event that you are thinking about a messy kitchen with remainders of canine food and a consuming oven —you can stop in that spot since that isn't what it will resemble. On the off chance that you plan your culinary action well, making these treats ought to be simple and simple to do.

Okay, let us start by recognizing what normal isn't. Normal dog treats don't infer taking care of your pet, something that became out of your tree patio or whatever it is that sprung out of the ground. While some might be beneficial for us, there are numerous things that will be adverse to the dog's framework when ingested.

A case of this would be the tomato plant. This is an amazing wellspring of nutrients without a doubt, yet it likewise contains atropine. Atropine, as found in higher focus in tomato stems and leaves, is known to result in enlarged understudies, quakes and flighty heartbeat for dogs. Abstain from serving dinners that have tomatoes in the recipes.

A portion of the natural product you have in your kitchen may likewise be destructive for him. Cherries, apples and apricots have seeds that contain cyanogenic glycosides. This can achieve cyanide harming, which obviously is risky for the creature. Grapes and avocados will prompt spewing and looseness of the bowels since they additionally contain dangerous substances that can seriously harm tissues and basic organs in the canine's body.

When searching for food to provide for your pet, consistently check the ingredients on the off chance that it contains the stuff that can hurt him. Try not to be disheartened by the number of things you can't utilize —there is a great deal more conceivable food to browse. You can make some extremely extraordinary tidbits when you get down to it. These indulgences are an amazing technique to remunerate him for good conduct and entirely executed orders.

Presently, what are a portion of the things you can give him? Most meat and fish are worthy (aside from salmon). Make a point to slash them up well to abstain from stifling occurrences. However, if you need to give organ meat like liver, do so, just in estimated sums.

Keep in mind homemade dog treats ought not to be a dreary and exhausting assignment. It ought to be entertaining! Blend in intriguing flavors and flavors for included energy. Be cautious about overloading the pet; however, so he doesn't hazard the risks that accompany weight. Plan and set up your pet's dinners well and find a healthy and upbeat dog when you do!

Healthy Herbal Homemade Dog Treats

Now that you feel like other dog sweethearts feel, your pet is thought of and dealt with like an individual from the family. Homemade dog treats are a brilliant method to show your affection. Your pet is similarly as imperative to you as the other relatives. You watched him develop from pup hood to a completely developed dog with a character, different preferences and returns unqualified love to you.

Similarly, as you avoid potential risk with your family's health by eating the correct foods, including healthy bites, you pay special mind to how you enjoy your pet too. It is the same amount of good times for pet guardians to give their pets homemade dog treats and healthy snacks for what it's worth for pets to eat them.

Tragically, most of the pet tidbits sold in stores are a long way from healthy. Indeed, huge numbers of them are made in China despite the fact that that reality isn't imprinted on the mark. Not many business pet tidbits bother to have the ingredients recorded on the name. You can be more than sure that additives are incorporated in addition to fillers that give the nibble more mass and make it taste great to the dog.

For instance, many dogs treat print, just the organization's name that is conveying the item. However, they don't state where the treat was initially prepared. If you notice that the standardized tag on the bundle has the initial three number successions of 690, 991 or 692, the item was made in China. What's so perilous about dog treats made in China?

Hartz —a main merchant of dog items in the US, as of late reviewed their Chicken Chews™ Soft and Tender and their Oinkies®Pig Skin Twists wrapped with Chicken since following measures of anti-toxin buildup was found. Obviously, Hartz isn't the main dog food merchant that needed to review items in view of pollution. More than 500 dogs passed on from eating jerky treats that contained glycerin from 2010 - 2012.

The best way to abstain from taking care of your dog's poison or ensuring that his bites are healthy for him is to make them yourself. Indeed, even void calories will inevitably add to his weight without giving any health benefit.

Dogs are rapacious, as proven by their teeth and short gastrointestinal frameworks. A few proprietors accept that they have a healthier eating routine because they feed their dog grains and vegetables, yet meat is fundamental for a balanced eating regimen. A decent treat for dogs that aren't perceived by most proprietors is any sort of genuine bone aside from chicken and turkey bones. Bones fulfill the need to bite, and their stomachs advantage from biting bones. You can buy bite bones at any butcher shop if you are a veggie lover.

If you need to make your own dog treats for preparing purposes or because you need to enjoy your pet, there are a few recipes everywhere on the Internet. If it's not too much trouble, know that a few creatures have sensitivities and watch your pet's response to treats that incorporate wheat, milk and eggs.

Cautioning: Never remember sugar for your pet's treats! Dogs can't deal with sugar.

Tips in Making Homemade Dog Food Treats

In the event that you are one of the many pet guardians who are worried about the sorts of foods that your dog eats, then it is significant that you make your own homemade dog treat recipes.

The recipes remembered for this book are healthy for your dogs. This part will concentrate on the tips and a stunt on making natural and common dog treats.

Interesting Points when making Doggie Treats

If you want to make dog treats, you probably won't get a decent response from your dog on the first occasion when you feed them with your homemade recipes. Indeed dogs resemble people as well, and they can be segregate about the kinds of foods they eat.

The following are what you have to consider when making doggie treats that your dog will doubtlessly eat.

Ingredients

The ingredients assume an imperative job in the by and large taste of the doggie treats. You must pick ingredients that are normal and natural. This is because dogs are sensitive to numerous sorts of foods. If your dog is adversely affected by one of the ingredients you are utilizing, you can generally fill in for healthier alternatives. For example, if your dog is hypersensitive to gluten or wheat, you can substitute wheat flour with rice flour, amaranth flour, quinoa flour, millet or corn starch.

Inclination

If your dog is likewise demanding about the sorts of food that it eats, then ensure that you make dog foods that the individual will probably eat. For example, on the off chance that your dog has a sweet tooth, make doggie treats that are likewise sweet yet just utilize normal wellsprings of sugar, such as nectar and fruit purée. Never put white sugar or counterfeit sugars on your homemade dog treats.

Calories

Focus on the number of calories that your dog is getting from your doggie treats. However, much as could reasonably be expected, don't overload your dog with treats. Indeed heftiness is a condition that generally influences numerous types of dogs. Just feed a few bits of treats every day to your dog.

Surface

Surface is significant in making dog treats. In the event that your dog isn't experiencing mature age, you have to take care of him with hard treats since it can make his teeth solid. In addition, giving hard doggie treats likewise helps wipe out the development of plaque.

Size

The best treats are those that can be taken in a solitary chomp. The best thing about giving little estimated homemade dog treats is ensuring that they are not eating an excessive amount of calories.

Capacity

Likewise, it is significant that you store your dog treats a similar way you would store treats expected for individuals. Keep it in a cool, dry and dim spot for treats or bread rolls. In the event that you get ready soft foods like biscuits or purees, ensure that you store them inside the ice chest. Whenever put away appropriately, your natural and common dog treats can keep going for as long as about fourteen days in a cool domain or two months inside the cooler.

Don't for Baking Doggie Snacks

Preparing homemade dog treat recipes is fun; however, imagine a scenario where it is your first time heating for your dog. Significantly, you think about the top don'ts in preparing doggie snacks. The following are the things that you ought to never do when preparing homemade dog treats.

Try not to Pick a Hard Formula

Never pick a hard formula if you have never at any point experienced heating any longer. Luckily, all recipes remembered for this book are extremely simple to follow, so they are exceptionally simple regardless of whether you are a first-time bread cook.

Try not to Utilize Ingredients that your Dog won't Care for

As the pet proprietor, it is significant that you comprehend what your dog enjoys and doesn't care to eat. Begin making dog treats utilizing ingredients that your dog likes.

Try not to utilize Ingredients that your Pet is Oversensitive to

Numerous dogs are hypersensitive to wheat. On the off chance that your dog is one of them, then substitute ingredients to something that your dog has no unfavorably susceptible response to.

Try not to Put all Ingredients Inside the Bowl

Follow the guide when making homemade dog treat recipes. Don't simply place all the ingredients in a single bowl. If you dump everything together, your dog treats won't end up being acceptable, as shown in the formula.

Try not to Expect for your Homemade Treats to Lat longer than Store Purchased Ones

Store-purchased doggie treats are weighed down with additives, so regardless of whether you store them out in the open, they can at present keep going for quite a while. Sadly, homemade dog treats can go mildew covered following seven days whenever put away at room temperature. Ensure that you make enough bunches that can keep going for seven days; otherwise, you will toss the extras away.

Try not to Take Care of your Dogs all Snacks in One Sitting

Your homemade treats may be healthy, yet it is as yet not a smart thought to take care of your dogs the entirety of the treats at a time. His treats ought to contain 10% of his eating regimen. Feed just three or four little parts of the doggie treats to your dog. This is sufficiently only to keep your dog glad.

33 Delicious Homemade Dog Treats Recipes

If you want to give your dogs a healthy gift, choose one of these great recipes!

1) <u>**CINNAMON DOGGIE BUN BITES**</u>

This tasty doggie bun bite has cinnamon that is very good for the dog's health. This is a treat that dogs will surely love.

<u>Ingredients:</u>

- ¼ cup of finely chopped walnuts
- 1 tea spoon of cinnamon
- 2 tablespoon of honey
- 1 large egg
- ¼ cup of canola oil
- ½ cup of water or milk
- ¼ tea spoon of salt
- 1 teaspoon of baking powder
- 2 cups of whole wheat flour

Steps:

1. In a bowl, combine the flour, salt and baking powder and mix well.

2. In a separate bowl, mix water, oil and egg and lightly beat the mixture.

3. Gradually add the wet ingredients to the flour mixture and blend well to form a soft dough.

4. Roll the dough on a floured surface and knead for a minute.

5. Make buns out of the dough and sprinkle the buns with honey, cinnamon and nuts.

6. Bake for 15 minutes or until the bun turns golden brown.

2) ICE PAWS TREAT

This icy dog treat is made from yogurt and tuna, which is something that your dog will surely like to nibble during a hot summer day.

Ingredients:

- 2 teaspoon of garlic powder
- 1 small can of tuna in water
- 2 cartons of plain vanilla

Steps:

1. Mix all of the ingredients in a bowl thoroughly.
2. Put the mixture on ice trays and freeze overnight.
3. Serve cold.

3) HOMEMADE MUTLOAF

This healthy doggie meatloaf recipe is loaded with lean meats and nutritious vegetables to make your dog active and maintain his or her healthy weight.

Ingredients:

- 1 tablespoon of olive oil
- 2 cloves of garlic
- ¼ cup of chopped zucchini
- ¼ cup of chopped spinach
- ¼ cup of chopped carrot ½ cup wheat germ
- 2 whole eggs
- ½ cup of cottage cheese
- 1 ½ lb of ground chicken

- 1 ½ cups of chicken broth ½ cup amaranth

Steps:

1. Add chicken broth and amaranth in a saucepan and bring the mixture to a boil.

2. Reduce the heat and simmer for another 20 minutes. Set aside and let it cool.

3. Preheat the oven to 350°Fahrenheit.

4. In a large mixing bowl, mix the eggs, meat, cottage cheese and vegetables.

5. Add the wheat germ and the cooled amaranth and olive oil.

6. Put the mixture in a loaf pan and bake for one hour or until it's done.

Note: If you cannot find amaranth, you can substitute it for barley.

4) TREATS FOR DOGS FISH

Different dogs have different preferences regarding the food they want to eat. If your dog likes to eat fish, then this homemade gift for dogs is for you. You can replace tuna with sardines.

Ingredients:

- Finely grated Parmesan 190 grams of whole meal flour

- 2 eggs

- 2 small tuna (drained)

Steps:

1. Preheat oven to 350^0 Fahrenheit.

2. Crush the fish in a bowl with a food processor and add the eggs and flour to get the biscuit mixture.

3. Pour the mixture on the baking sheet and lightly sprinkle with parmesan.

4. Bake for 5 minutes until the edges narrow from the sides of the muffin tray.

5) **DOGGIE TRAIL MIX**

The mix of trails is not only appreciated by humans. Combine the remaining grains from your fridge to create a delicious mix of trails. It is better to have fun if you take your dog to the park.

Ingredients:

- Dried Fruits (not raisins or grapes), vegetables (zucchini, carrots and peas), potatoes

- Remaining pieces of meat (rinse any flavor)

Steps:

1. Cut all ingredients to ½ inch thick part.

2. Mix everything in a bowl and put everything in a food dehydrator until dry.

3. Frozen peanut butter and yogurt treats

4. It is a perfect snack to refresh your dog during the summer after a fun session.

6) YOGURT

Ingredients:

- 1 cup of peanut butter

- 32 oz of natural yogurt

Steps:

1. Melt the peanut butter in a microwave oven.

2. Once dissolved, pour the yogurt into the bowl and mix everything.

3. Pour the mixture into cupcake cards.

4. Put in the refrigerator to solidify.

7) **THE SWEET KISS COOKIE**

This homemade gift for dogs is made of ingredients that your dog will definitely appreciate. Persil also comes with parsley, which is rich in vitamins C and A. In addition, parsley can also help maintain good digestion and keeps your breath sweet at all times for the name to go.

Ingredients:

- 1 cup of peanut butter

- ½ Cup of skimmed milk

- ½ Cup of water

- 2 large eggs

- 1 tablespoon of Persil dried leaves

- 1 cup of oat flakes

- 2 cups of whole meal flour

Steps:

1. Preheat the oven to 300⁰Fahrenheit.

2. Mix all the dry ingredients in a large bowl.

3. In another bowl, whisk the eggs and add water and peanut butter. Mix well to incorporate wet ingredients.

4. Combine dry and wet ingredients.

5. Mix well, and be sure to remove all the Tufts.

6. Knead the dough with your hands.

7. Take a rolling pin and flatten the dough on a flat surface.

8. Use a cookie cutter and cut cute bone shapes into the dough.

9. Bake for 30 minutes or until the cookies are golden brown.

10. Let cool to harden before feeding treatment for your dog.

8) **BAKED CUPCAKES WITH PEANUT BUTTER**

Peanut butter is a healthy food to feed your dog. It is a good source of protein, vitamins, and minerals. Many homemade recipes for dogs use peanut butter as the main ingredient, including these healthy peanut butter treats.

Ingredients:

- 1 ¼ cup of hot water
- 1/3 cup peanut butter 1 cup oatmeal
- 2 cups of whole meal flour

Steps:

1. Preheat the oven to 350 degrees Fahrenheit.

2. In a mixing bowl, combine all the ingredients and mix well to form a dough.

3. Knead the dough on a flat working surface.

4. Use a roller pin to flatten the dough and cut the desired shapes.

5. Put the cookies on a baking sheet covered with parchment paper. Do not use cooking spray as it is not healthy for your dog.

6. Cook for 30 minutes or until golden brown.

9) **PINK PLEASURE COOKIES**

They say that dogs are color-blind, but due to their incredible smell, they will be able to feel the rainbow goodness of this simple cookie recipe of pink delights. When making these cookies, be sure not to use artificial dyes because food dyes are very dangerous for dogs.

Ingredients:

- ½ Cup of a strawberry jam without sugar
- ½ Cup of water
- ½ Cup of low sodium chicken broth
- ½ Cup of peanut butter
- 2 teaspoons of cinnamon
- ½ Cup of oat flakes
- 2 cups of whole meal flour

Steps:

1. Beat oats, cinnamon, and flour in a bowl.

2. In another bowl, mix peanut butter, flour, strawberry jam and chicken broth and microwave for 15 seconds.

3. Pour wet ingredients gradually dry ingredients. Mix well with a fork until a soft dough is formed.

4. Take the rounded balls from the dough and put them on a baking sheet covered with parchment paper.

5. Bake at 3250 Fahrenheit in a preheated oven for 15 minutes or gold.

Note: Strawberry jam gives the cookies their pink color. If you do not have strawberry jam, you can omit this ingredient and proceed to the preparation of the dough. It can also be replaced with other berries, including blueberries without bones.

10) IRREGULAR MEAT

This dry meat recipe is a great way to keep your dog busy. It's also a great way to train him not to chew your stuff. Here is a great organic and natural dog treat that you can give to your canine friend.

Ingredients:

- 1 cup of beef liver
- 1 minced meat

Steps:

1. Cut the liver into small pieces and mix them with minced meat.

2. Collect the meat and put it in a bowl.

3. Pressure gun to form pressure sheets. If you do not have a gun, you can flatten the meat before putting it in the dehydrator.

4. Set the dehydrator to 1650 Fahrenheit for three to four hours until the meat becomes crispy.

11) CHICKEN COOKIES DOGGY STYLE

Chicken is a good source of lean protein. Use this homemade dog treats recipe to create delicious cookies for your dogs.

Ingredients:

- 1 cup of cornflour
- 2 cups of whole meal flour
- 3 eggs, lightly beaten
- 3 tablespoons of coconut oil
- ½ cup of chicken broth
- 1 lb chopped chicken meat

Steps:

1. In a saucepan, put the water and chicken soil.

2. Put the mixture in the blender. Add the eggs and olive oil and mix until the mixture is incorporated.

3. Pour the mixture into a bowl and add flour and corn flour.

4. Put the spoons of the mixture on sheets of cookies covered with parchment paper.

5. Bake for 20 minutes in a preheated oven to 4500 degrees Fahrenheit.

6. Let the cookies cool before giving it to your dog.

12) APPLE AND CINNAMON COOKIES

Cinnamon and apples are excellent food for dogs suffering from arthritis and gout. It is a high fiber food that comes with many vitamins and minerals so that your older dog can still get the nutrients it needs to stay healthy at his age.

Ingredients:

- 2 large organic eggs
- ½ Cup of milk powder (can be replaced with wheat cream)
- 5 cups of brown rice flour
- ½ Cup of olive oil
- 1 cup of cold water
- 1 table spoon of Persil
- 1 tea spoon of cinnamon
- 1 cup of organic apple compote

Steps:

1. Mix all the ingredients until the Tufts are no longer formed.

2. Knead the dough on a flat working surface.

3. Roll out the dough and cover with a plastic wrap.

4. Refrigerate the dough for 1.5 hours or overnight.

5. Flatten the dough with a rolling pin and cut the desired shape the next day.

6. Bake 30 minutes in the oven at 350 degrees Fahrenheit or until golden brown.

7. Let it cool until it hardens.

13) **VEGETARIAN MUFFINS FOR PUPPIES**

If your dog does not like to eat your vegetables, then this vegetarian gift will make your puppy eat vegetables. This treatment is a great way to add more nutritional value to what your dog eats. It is also an excellent treatment to give to dogs suffering from obesity.

Ingredients:

- ¾ cup of whole flour
- ¼ cup of dry oats
- 1 cup off lax seed
- ¼ cup of water
- ¼ cup of molasses (plus 2 extra tablespoons if needed)
- 2 cups of grated carrots
- 1 peeled and 1 chopped apples

Steps:

1. Mix all the ingredients in a bowl.

2. Lightly butter the muffin molds and put enough dough into the muffin molds.

3. Bake for 15 minutes at 400 Fahrenheit preheated or until golden brown.

4. Allow it to cool before giving a gift to your dog.

14) **VEGGIE TREAT FOR PUPPY**

This vegetarian dog treat is an excellent source of vitamins and minerals for your dog. It is low in fat and phosphorus, which makes it ideal for dogs with limited dietary requirements and those who suffer from obesity.

Ingredients:

- ½ Cup of cold water

- 6 table spoons of low-sodium vegetable broth

- 1 teaspoon of dried Persil

- 1 cup of cooked vegetables

- 2 ½ cups rice flour (can be replaced with brown rice flour)

Steps:

1. In a large bowl, mix all the dry ingredients and mix well. Shelve.

2. In another bowl, mix the wet ingredients and gradually add them to the dry ingredients.

3. Remove all the Tufts from the dough.

4. Knead the dough on a flat surface and cut the desired shapes.

5. Place the treats on a baking sheet covered with parchment paper.

6. Bake for 25 minutes in a preheated oven at 350 degrees Fahrenheit.

15) **<u>MASHED LIVER AND CARROT</u>**

This dog puree treatment is ideal for older dogs. It is a good source of iron, beta carotene and vitamins and minerals. As it is already crushed, it does not overload the stomach of old dogs, so they do not have indigestion with this treatment.

<u>Ingredients:</u>

- 1 lb liver, chopped 1/3 cup grated carrots
- 1 egg
- 1 ½ whole wheat flour
- 1 cup of corn flour
- 1 tea spoon of oregano

Steps:

- Mix the wheat flour, corn flour and oregano.

- Add the other ingredients to the flour mixture and mix well.

- Pour the dough into a pan covered with baking paper and bake for 30 minutes in an oven preheated to 350 degrees Fahrenheit.

- When cooling, cut the liver and vegetable puree into squares.

Do you think it involves too much time and hassle preparing homemade treats for your dog? Well, think again. Here are five quick and easy, delicious healthy home dog treats recipes for easy home dog treats that your dog will find irresistible!

16) **DELICIOUS PUPPY CHIPS**

Ingredients:

- 1 large potato

Steps:

1. Preheat the oven to 350 F.

2. Peel the potato and cut it into 1/3 inch thick pieces.

3. Put the slices on a greased baking sheet.

4. Cook for 2 hours.

Tip: If you cut them 1/3 inch thick, the center will be slightly spongy, but you can also try cutting them thinner to turn them into crispy delicacies.

17) **TASTY MEATBALLS**

Ingredients:

- 1 lb. of minced meat
- 4 table spoons of grated Parmesan
- 2 grated carrots
- 1 cup of bread crumbs
- 2 beaten eggs

Steps:

1. Preheat the oven to 350 F.

2. Mix all the ingredients and mix well, then roll up the meatballs.

3. Put on a well-oiled baking sheet.

4. Cook for 15-20 minutes, or until golden brown and soda.

5. Store in a refrigerator to keep cool. Unused delicacies can be frozen for freshness.

18) LUSH FROZEN CARROT COOLERS

Ingredients:

- 32oz. of natural yogurt
- 2 cups of carrots cooked, crushed and cooled.

Steps:

1. Combine the ingredients in a bowl and mix well.
2. Pour the mixture into ice trays.
3. Freeze overnight.

19) **EASY CHEESY**

Ingredients:

- 1/2 cups of whole meal flour

- 3/4 cups of grated cheddar cheese

- 1 bar of margarine

Steps:

1. Preheat the oven to 350 F.

2. Mix the cheese, margarine and flour.

3. It is formed into 2 trunks about 2 inches wide.

4. Cool in the refrigerator.

5. Cut into 1/4 inch thick slices and put on a greased baking sheet

6. Cook for 15-20 minutes, or until golden brown and soda.

7. Allow it to cool completely before serving.

20) FROZEN PEANUT BUTTER

Ingredients:

- 1 cup of vanilla yogurt (32oz)
- 1 cup of peanut butter

Steps:

1. Microwave peanut butter in a safe dish until it melts.

2. Mix the melted peanut butter and yogurt in a bowl.

3. Take the mixture and pour it into the cupcake cards and freeze.

21) **MEAT BISCUITS**

Ingredients:

- 6 jar of beef and vegetables for babies
- 1 cup of wheat germ
- 2 cups of skimmed milk

Steps:

1. Preheat oven to 350.

2. Take all the ingredients and mix them in a large bowl.

3. Take small spoons of the mixture and place it in a greased pan.

4. If desired, flatten them slightly or cut into more fun shapes such as legs, bones, etc.

5. Bake for about 12-15 minutes until brown at the edges. Let stand until cool.

6. Store in a refrigerator.
7. Serve your pet and let them enjoy it.

22) **CARROT COOKIES**

Ingredients:

- 2 cups of carrots (mashed or boiled)

- 2 eggs

- 2 table spoons of chopped garlic

- 2 cups of raw flour (or rice flour)

- 1 cup of oat flake

- 1/4 cup of wheat germ

Steps:

1. Mix garlic, carrots and eggs. Stir until smooth. Add the remaining ingredients.

2. Roll the contents onto a tightly floured surface.

3. Cut them into shapes or bars. Set the oven to 300 degrees for 45 minutes.

4. As it cools, the center hardens. To give it a glossy finish, brush with egg white before cooking.

The best move when switching the dog to homemade treats is to do it slowly as possible. Always prepare vegetables by cooking or smoking so they can retain their nutrients. And remember, like humans, dogs also need a certain amount of protein and fiber to maintain health.

23) **VEGGIE BAGELS**

This veggie bagel formula is stacked with a great deal of vegetables that are acceptable wellsprings of strands, nutrients and minerals. You can give your dogs the bagels as they or you can slather it with a decent measure of nutty spread to make it more flavorful.

Ingredients:

- ½cupofcarrots, hacked

- ½cupofspinach, hacked

- ¼ teaspoon of heating powder

- 1 egg

- ¼ teaspoon preparing soft drink

- 1 teaspoon of vegetable oil

- ½cupofwheat flour

- 2 ½ cups of white flour

- ¾ cup of water

Steps:

1. Combine all the dry ingredients in a blending bowl.

2. On a different bowl, include the dry ingredients. Blend until the entirety of the ingredients is all around mixed.

3. Gradually add the wet ingredients to the dry ingredients and blend.

4. Shape little round bundles of mixture and jab openings in the batter.

5. Place the bagel balls in a preheated broiler and cook for 45 minutes at 300 Fahrenheit.

24) NUTTY SPREAD AND BANANA DOGGIE BISCUITS

There are numerous uncommon homemade dog treat recipes that you can attempt, and one of them is this unique veggie-lover doggie diet.

This specific formula is incredible for senior dogs that are experiencing kidney and liver illnesses. It is a low-fat treat that, despite everything, has similar goodness as other rich doggie treats out there.

Ingredients:

- ½ tea spoon of cinnamon
- 1 ¼ cup of entire wheat flour
- ½ cup of fruit purée
- 1 cup of oats
- ½ cup nutty spread

- 1 squashed banana

Steps:

1. In a blending bowl, combine the entirety of the ingredients to shape a soft mixture.

2. Knead the mixture on a level surface for a few minutes.

3. Let it cool before smoothing, utilizing a moving pin.

4. Cut out the ideal states of the doggie scones.

5. Place the doggie scones on a heating sheet fixed with material paper.

6. Bake in a 350 Fahrenheit preheated broiler for 15 minutes or until the edges become brilliant.

7. Let the treats cool before putting them away in the cooler.

25) YAM BISCUITS

This yam dog scone isn't just normally sweet; however, it is likewise wealthy in fiber, potassium, and cell reinforcements that can improve your dog's general health.

Ingredients:

- 1 egg, softly beaten

- 1 ¾ cup of entire wheat flour (can be subbed with earthy colored rice flour) 1 cup yam, pounded

Steps:

1. Preheat the broiler to 350 Fahrenheit.

2. Mix all ingredients in an enormous bowl to shape a soft mixture.

3. Roll the mixture into little balls and spot them on a treat sheet fixed with material paper.

4. Press the batter, so the bread rolls are ¼ inch thick.

5. Bake until brilliant earthy colored and let them cool on a wire rack.

26) **SPINACH TREAT**

This is a healthy treat that you can provide for your dog. This is particularly obvious on the off chance that you need your dog to get thinner.

Ingredients:

- ½teaspoon of heating powder
- 2 ½ cups of entire wheat flour
- ½cup of fruit purée
- ¼ cup of unsweetened plain yogurt
- ¾ cup blended vegetables (cauliflower, broccoli and carrots)
- 1 cup of new infant spinach

Steps:

1. Preheat the broiler to 350Fahrenheit.

2. Dice the spinach and the blended vegetables in a food processor.

3. Put the diced vegetables in a huge bowl.

4. Add the yogurt and fruit purée to the veggie blend.

5. In a medium bowl, mix together the preparing powder and flour.

6. Mix the ingredients together to frame the batter.

7. Knead the batter until a firm ball is accomplished

8. Flatten the batter with a folding pin and cut it into shapes with a cutout.

9. Place the treats on a preparing sheet fixed with material paper.

10. On a different bowl, blend yogurt and water.

11. Lightly brush the treat batter with the yogurt blend.

12. Bake on the stove for 20 minutes.

13. Let it cool before taking care of your dog.

27) HOMEMADE LIVER BROWNIES

Dogs do experience the ill effects of sickliness as well, and these homemade liver brownies. This liver brownie is a decent wellspring of Vitamin an and protein, which are useful for your dog's health.

Ingredients:

- ½ cup of dried parsley
- 2 ½ teaspoon of granulated garlic
- 2eggs
- 2cups of wheat germ
- 2cupsofcorn dinner
- 2lbofchicken liver

Steps:

1. Put the liver inside the food processor and add the other ingredients to make a smooth surface.
2. Spread the liver blend on a treat sheet fixed with material paper.
3. Bake for 350 Fahrenheit for about 35 minutes.
4. Let it cool and cut into squares.
5. Place inside a zip lock sack and store inside the cooler.

28) LOW-FAT SPINACH DOGGIE BALLS

In the event that your dog is extra stout, then this low-fat spinach doggie balls is an extraordinary bite to hold your dog's weight under tight restraints.

Ingredients:

- 1 tea spoon of dried oregano
- 2 tablespoon of ground Parmesan cheddar
- ¾ cup of moved oats
- ¾ cup of entire wheat flour
- 1 tablespoon of olive oil
- 1 cup of cleaved spinach

Steps:

1. Preheat the stove to 350 Fahrenheit.

2. Mix together spinach and olive oils in a bowl.

3. In a different bowl, combine the flour, cheddar, oats and oregano.

4. Make a well at the focal point of the flour blend and include the spinach.

5. Stir until it frames a soft batter.

6. Knead the batter on a floured surface and level it utilizing a moving pin.

7. Use a treat scooper and make adjusted balls and spot them on a preparing sheet fixed with material paper.

8. Bake in the broiler for 30 minutes or until brilliant earthy colored.

29) APPLE CARROT TREATS

These apple carrot dog munchies are wealthy in fiber and beta-carotene. It is an extraordinary doggie nibble for dogs that adoration sweet treats.

It is an extraordinary nibble for dogs that experience the ill effects of heftiness.

Ingredients:

- ½ cup of unsweetened fruit purée
- 1 egg
- 1 cup of ground carrots
- 1 cup of earthy colored rice flour

Steps:

1. Preheat the broiler to 350 Fahrenheit.

2. In a bowl, blend all the ingredients to shape a mixture.

3. Roll the mixture utilizing a moving pin and make little balls utilizing your hands.

4. Place the little mixture on a treat sheet fixed with material paper.

5. Flatten the mixture utilizing a fork.

6. Bake for 15 minutes or until brilliant earthy colored.

30) **DELICIOUS PEANUT BUTTER BALLS**

Ingredients:

- 1 cup of milk
- 2 eggs
- 4 table spoons of peanut butter
- 2 tablespoons of water
- 1/2 tea spoon of salt
- 1/2 cup of flour

Steps:

1. Preheat the oven to 350 F.

2. Combine all the ingredients in a large bowl and mix well with your hands.

3. Roll into bite-sized balls and put them on a greased biscuit plate.

4. Cook for 15-20 minutes.

5. Store in an airtight container in the refrigerator. Freeze all unused delicacies for optimal freshness.

31) PUMPKIN PUREE PERFECTION

Pumpkin is very nutritious for dogs and is loaded with vitamins E and C and other antioxidants. In addition, the high fiber content in the pumpkin is also ideal for maintaining a healthy weight for your dogs. The beta carotene contained in pumpkin is also good for reducing cataracts and heart problems in your dogs.

Ingredients:

- ½ cup of milk powder
- ¾ Cup of wheat cream
- 15 of oz raw pumpkin, puree

Steps:

1. In a bowl, mix all the ingredients and mix well.
2. Place the ingredients on a baking sheet.
3. Bake in the oven at 3000 Fahrenheit for 15 minutes.
4. Allow it to cool before serving your dog.

32) **SUNFLOWER DOG BISCUITS**

Ingredients:

- 2 cups of Flour
- 1/3 cup of Cereal
- ½ cups of Shelled Sunflower Seeds
- 2 tablespoons of Flaxseed oil
- ½ cup of Chicken Broth
- 2 whole Eggs-blended in with ¼ Cup milk
- 1 whole Egg-beaten
- 2 tsp. New Mint (common breath purifier)

Steps:

1. Preheat stove to 350 degrees. In an enormous bowl, combine the flour, oats and seeds. Include oil, chicken stock and egg and milk blend.

2. Let rest for 30 minutes. Then, pour onto a floured surface and turn out until ¼" thick. Utilize your decision of cutout and brush with the beaten egg for a pleasant gleam.

3. Prepare for 30 min until brilliant. Let it cool off.

4. Enjoy your dog with the awesome kind of a homemade treat.

33) PUMPKIN DOG TREAT RECIPE

Ingredients:

- 15 oz. of pounded unadulterated cooked pumpkin

- 3/4 cup of cereal. You can blend this dry — no compelling reason to cook it first

- 1/2 cup of dry powdered milk

Steps:

1. Preheat broiler to 300 F.

2. Combine all ingredients. Drop little spoonfuls (I use about a portion of a tablespoon) onto a softly lubed treat sheet and heat at 300 degrees for 15-20 minutes.

3. On the off chance that you'd prefer to make reduced down treats for little dogs, preparing rewards or simply little treats, you can utilize a cake pack and crush out rosettes about the size of a huge catch for delicious scaled-down treats!

4. Contingent upon the size, this formula will make around 20 treats. This healthy homemade dog treat is ideal for preparing or outright treating your unique companion.

Homemade Dog Treats Vs Store Bought

Homemade treats: Homemade treats have loads of focal points for your dog. You can utilize any ingredients you and your dog like. In the event that he has a few inclinations like, for instance, blueberries, you can make him blueberry treats or doggy biscuits with blueberries. Heaps of extraordinary treat recipes for fish treats and fish treats for dogs on the off chance that he is obsessed with fish. You can give him precisely what he loves best.

With homemade treats you can control the nature of the ingredients, as well. You can utilize similar ingredients that you would use for your own family. You realize the ingredients are healthy and ok for your dog. You can likewise utilize natural ingredients in the event that you like or purchase from nearby ranchers.

You can likewise deliver similarly the same number of or as not many of the treats as you need to make. You can use fourfold a formula and make loads of treats so you can freeze them. Or then again, you can cause a little clump to perceive how your dog likes them. By and large, when you make treats yourself, you will wind up setting aside cash since you can purchase ingredients in mass or when they are discounted.

If your dog has hypersensitivities, you can ensure that you just use ingredients that are ok for your dog to eat and abstain from utilizing any things that may trigger a response in your dog.

What's more, homemade treats are typically flavorful. Dogs will adore them. You can give him treats directly out of the broiler. Nothing says, "I love you," very like preparing for your dog.

Store-bought treats: There are some extraordinary, locally acquired treats, as well. Obviously, some business treats have flawed ingredients, and you will most likely need to keep away from them, similarly as there are some lower quality dog foods. You ought to stay away from treats that utilization creature condensation or bi-items, for instance. Yet, trustworthy organizations make some awesome treats that utilize human evaluation ingredients, natural ingredients, and which have great notorieties. These would surely be acceptable treats to give your dog.

Three Dog Bakery makes great treats utilizing regular ingredients for dogs with numerous innovative flavors. Old Mother Hubbard is an organization that has been around for quite a while and is known for making healthy treats utilizing human evaluation ingredients for dogs, and there are others. On the off chance that you feed your dog a decent quality dog food, the organization that makes the food presumably makes dog treats, as well, so check the store to check whether they convey them.

End

If you have the opportunity to make homemade dog treats for your dog, your dog will cherish them.

They are consistently brilliant. In any case, on the off chance that you don't have time or on the off chance that you prefer not to heat, don't feel awful.

There are still some excellent locally acquired dog treats that your dog will cherish.

Printed in Great Britain
by Amazon